MW00906350

PENSKE SUPPORTS THE
GREATER READING CHAMBER'S
WOMEN IN BUSINESS INITIATIVES.

Ready Set Plan Go!
Strategies to Accelerate Your Success
COMPLIMENTS OF

READY
SET
PLAN
GO!

READY
SET
PLN
GO!

STRATEGIES TO ACCELERATE YOUR SUCCESS

JOAN WALSH

WOOL STREET PUBLISHING

Georgia

Copyright@2007 by Joan Walsh

All rights reserved.
Printed in the United States of America
No part of this book may be reproduced or utilized in any
form or by any means, electronic or mechanical, including
photocopying, recording, or by any information storage
retrieval system, without permission in writing from
the copyright owner.

Cover Design: Paul Fusch – http://www.macabooart.com

Cataloging-in-Publication data is on file with
The Library of Congress

ISBN-10: 0-9797422-0-X
ISBN-13: 978-0-9797422-0-0

Published by Wool Street Publishing

This book is available at special quantity discounts
to use as premiums and sales promotions,
or for use in corporate training programs.
For additional copies or more information, please contact

Wool Street Publishing
133 Worthing Road
Saint Simons Island, GA 31522
912.634.5777

For Tim, the funniest man I know

CONTENTS

Acknowledgements . . . . *ix*
Introduction . . . . *xi*

READY

1. Stuck in the Starting Blocks? 3
2. How's Your Life Right Now? 11
3. You Can Do It! 29

SET

4. What's Your Passion? 41
5. Are You in Shape? 55
6. Where's the Finish Line? 69

PLAN

7. Planning the Race. 81
8. Keeping Your Balance. 91

GO!

9. A Winning Attitude 99
10. Passing the Baton. 111
11. Drawing Strength from the Crowd. 123
12. Pacing Yourself 133
13. Standing on the Podium. 143

APPENDIX

I   How a Coach Can Help 147
II Recommended Resources. 151

About the Author *158*
About the Company *159*
Contact Information *160*
Journal *161*

Acknowledgements

A very special group of people deserve "gold medals" for their contributions to this project and to me.

The first gold medal goes to the guy who challenged me more than once to put pen to paper. David Herdlinger (www.TheCoach.biz), your wise counsel, experience, continuing support, and absolute belief made all the difference. You are always there for me, and for that I am grateful.

Michael Dowling (www.MichaelJDowling.com), you deserve a gold medal for the way you have enriched this project with your exceptional writing and editing skills. You provided a first-time author everything she could ask for.

Step up on the top tier of the podium, Paul Fusch (www.macabooart.com) and Jerry Dorris (www. AuthorSupport.com). Paul, your cover design is truly a knock-out winner. And Jerry, your outstanding interior design and layout add immeasurably to the readability and attractiveness of the book.

Allow me to hang a gold medal around your neck, Sue Frantz. As my expert administrative assistant, you provided valuable input, editing, and coordination of this project from the start right through to publication. Your speed, accuracy, and thoroughness dazzle me.

To my colleagues who read drafts and provided valuable input, thank you!

The last and most important medals go to the three guys behind the scenes: my husband, Tim, and my sons, Bobby and Brian. With patience and understanding you supported and encouraged me as I was giving birth to this book. I love you!

Introduction

As a business coach, I've had the privilege over
the years of working with hundreds of executives,
managers, entrepreneurs, and business owners at
all organizational levels and in a wide variety of
industries. Unfortunately, I've noticed that many of
them are enjoying less satisfaction and success than
they desire, both personally and professionally.

Why are so many business professionals strug-

gling? Many reasons come to mind – fear, indeci-
siveness, wrong priorities – the list goes on. But
two major causes seem to predominate.

⊙ Many of them don't know what they want. In
other words, they're not living their passion.

⊙ Even those who know where they're going
often don't know how to get there; they don't
have plans.

People who are not passionate about where
they're going usually aren't going very far. And
people who fail to plan are planning to fail.

Conversely, when individuals discover what
they truly want and develop plans to get there,
they generally achieve more than they previously
thought possible. And when businesses develop
sound plans, set clear goals, and assemble teams
with the right skills and attitudes, they almost
invariably exceed their goals.

I love to help individuals and organizations transform their perceptions, attitudes, and
behaviors so they can grow to their full potential.
That's why I'm a business coach, and that's why
I've written this book. It's a practical guide to strategies for personal and professional success.

The personal testimonies in the book are true.

Although I've changed the names and some details to protect confidentiality, the essential facts are accurate. I hope they encourage you.

If you're stuck in one or more areas of your life, you will benefit from the insights in this book. Use it as a continuing resource to refer to again and again. Complete the helpful exercises. Take advantage of the additional resources listed in Appendix II.

This book is not just a collection of nice ideas. It's a distillation of powerful, field-tested principles that will positively transform your life, both personally and professionally. I've seen them work in people's lives, and I'm confident they'll work in yours too.

I'm thrilled that you've picked up this book. It's truly an honor to join you on your journey toward extraordinary success and fulfillment.

READY

Chapter One:

Stuck In The Starting Blocks

I magine you're watching an Olympic hundred-meter dash. Can you visualize the scene? The runners are pacing nervously around the starting area, stretching.

"Ready," calls the starting official.

The runners carefully place their feet in the starting blocks and crouch into their starting positions.

"Set."

Like coiled springs they wait, eyes focused on the finish line. The starting pistol is poised high in the air.

BANG!

They're off! Finely tuned bodies in a blur of motion catapult down the track.

But wait! One runner is still stuck in the blocks. He hasn't moved! There's something…could it be glue, or flypaper, or something…holding him back.

* * *

What if that really happened? How would you react? I suspect I'd be inclined to laugh. What a funny scene – a runner stuck in the blocks!

But then I'd empathize with that poor runner. I wouldn't want that to happen to me, or to anyone I know.

Unfortunately, something similar does happen to many of us at different times in our lives. We get stuck and we can't seem to get traction. But I'm thankful that I'm often able to help people in this situation, because I'm a business coach.

As a coach, I delight in helping people leap over the hurdles that threaten to keep them from winning in life. It thrills me to see my clients unleash their potential and catapult toward their goals.

YOU'RE NOT ALONE

Are you stuck in the starting blocks, either personally or professionally? Are you putting out lots of effort for very little accomplishment and satisfaction? If so, maybe you can identify with some of these people I know.

Roger has been in the financial services field for more than forty years, and has been the president of his own firm for fifteen. As he sat across the desk from me, tears came to his eyes. "I'm sixty years old, and this business is not where it should be. It's not growing, and I don't know how to make it grow. One day last week five of my employees were out sick. I feel frustrated and overwhelmed. Maybe I should just retire, but that's not what I really want."

I'll tell you the rest of Roger's story later in the book. He became a client, and the ending is happier than the beginning. But first, allow me to introduce you to some more people I know.

George was successfully engaged in research for a company that develops and markets food products. Suddenly one of his two partners died, and he had to move into marketing and management. But George didn't know how to run a business. He didn't know how to develop a plan and move forward. He felt paralyzed.

* * *

Teresa develops new business for a construction company of about fifty employees. She wanted to be more successful, but she was hindered by her boss's refusal to develop a business plan. "I don't know where the company's going," she admitted, "and I don't know where I'm going."

* * *

Ralph is a manager for a company with $1 billion in annual sales, and he's underperforming. Actually, he doesn't like his job, but he earns over $200,000 per year. He's unhappy, but he's afraid to leave.

I'll reintroduce you to all of these folks later, in Chapter 3, and give you the rest of their stories. You'll find them encouraging.

HOW ABOUT YOU?

Do you relate to any of their predicaments? Are you stuck in situations that cause you tremendous frustration? Do you feel as if you're running like crazy and getting nowhere? Are some things demanding lots of your attention, while other more important goals and desires suffer from neglect?

When people ask me to be their coach, they are typically acting out of either desperation or inspiration. The desperate ones often are in anguish and pain. They're stuck in situations they can't tolerate much longer. They know they need to change and they want to change, but they need help.

Others come to me out of inspiration. They are inspired to take their lives to the next level. They're doing well, but they know they can do better. They're not satisfied with "good enough." They want to be the best they can be.

If you're in either of those categories, I wrote this book for you. It combines sound principles with exercises and real-life examples to make it as practical as possible. I hope you'll not just read it once, but that you'll use it as a reference to make sure you stay on track throughout your life.

BURIED TREASURE

There's another category of people I encounter. This group doesn't see the need for change because they've become numb to the pain. Perhaps because they don't think change is possible, they've pushed their hearts' desires down below the conscious level. On the outside they may appear to be doing OK, but inside they have little or no passion and joy. I call them "nummies."

How do I know about this group of nummies? First, statistics consistently show that 60 percent to 70 percent of American workers are unhappy in their jobs. Imagine that! Two out of every three workers almost certainly are performing below their potential and settling for less accomplishment and satisfaction than they should.

Second, from published research and from my experiences as a coach, I know that most people struggle with attaining balance in their lives. Pressures from work cause them to short-change their personal lives, and vice versa. Demands from multiple directions leave them feeling tense, guilty, cheated, and frustrated.

I encourage you to use the exercises in the next chapter to help you look beneath the surface.

When you dig down deep, you may uncover a buried treasure – your passion. Perhaps you'll realize that you desire something different, but that you've been suppressing your desire because you didn't think change was possible. If you're a "nummie," I wrote this book for you, too.

FACING CHANGE

All changes are inconvenient; some changes are scary; a few changes are even risky. As you proceed through this book and spot areas that need change, you will confront some barriers that are within you. You will come face to face with your own values, attitudes, disappointments, and fears.

You may find that you need to change your circumstances in order to achieve your goals. Such change usually requires courage, wisdom, and perseverance. You also may realize that you have to change yourself. That always requires courage, wisdom, and perseverance…and usually some humility, as well.

Why humility? Because in order to change, you need to admit to yourself, and often to some others, that you're stuck. And more than likely you'll need to ask for help. It's difficult to see ourselves clearly and objectively. In order to move beyond the blocks that hinder our success, we usually need the insights and encouragement of other people.

Remember Ralph, the unhappy manager who earns more than $200,000 a year? In order to bring fulfillment into his life, he may have to be willing to give up the perceived security of that lucrative job. He may have to take risks and change his values. That's a difficult assignment, especially alone.

I strongly believe you will be most successful and most fulfilled when you are living your passion. You will attain the most significant accomplishments when your passion and your goals are aligned.

I hope this book inspires you to find your passion and go for it. I hope it helps you discover what you were created to do and do it!

The sign on the door of opportunity reads PUSH.

AUTHOR UNKNOWN

Chapter Two

How's Your Life Right Now?

When you're running a race, you have to start at the starting line. When you're running your life, you have to start where you are.

Sometimes it's difficult to *identify* where you are. A coach, a good friend, or a trusted business associate can help you view your life more objectively. Assessment tools and exercises, such as the ones in this chapter, can also help increase your awareness and clarify your perspective.

Sometimes it's difficult to *acknowledge* where you are. If you're stuck in the starting blocks in one or more areas of your life, it often takes courage to admit it. But truth is the starting point for progress.

In this chapter you will have an opportunity to reflect on your life in order to get a sense of where you are compared to where you want to be. You'll look at the important facets of your personal life: family, career, finances, health, learning, spiritual, social, and civic. And you'll assess the key components of your professional life.

You may realize that you're not entirely where you want to be. But remember, no matter where you are now, you can chart a course that will take you toward the destination you desire.

The only place to start is at the starting line. So for best results, be honest with yourself as you complete the exercises in the remainder of this chapter. They'll help you establish where you are. Subsequent chapters will set you off and running toward where you want to be.

WHAT'S YOUR PROFILE?

Admittedly, your answers to these exercises will be subjective. To a significant degree, however, your subjective feelings represent reality to you. You are not really successful if you don't feel successful. If you are not satisfied with how an area of your life is progressing, you will still want to work on that area, even if only to change your attitude about it.

It's usually unrealistic, even undesirable, to try to focus maximum attention on all areas. During some seasons of your life you may need to devote more attention to your professional life, while somewhat neglecting areas of your personal life. At other times, personal issues may demand attention that you normally would prefer to devote to professional goals. Life is a dynamic process, and your answers to these exercises will reflect that.

Besides, no one is equally interested or gifted in all areas. For example, if you are currently focused on starting a business or sending kids to college, you may have to let your social life slide a bit. That's not to say your social life isn't important to you, but right now other things may demand higher priority.

You may not be totally pleased with your current

profile, and that's fine. The important thing is to identify the areas that you want to work on in order to put you on the path to where you want to be. So let's get started by completing some exercises that will help you find the starting line.

EXERCISE #1

For each of the areas listed on the next several pages, indicate how you think you're doing today by shading in the graphs. How much of your time, energy, and talent are you devoting to each area? How much of your potential are you realizing in each area? How effective are your efforts in producing the positive results you want?

To help you arrive at your answers, I've presented two opposing descriptions – one positive and one negative. Most of the time you'll probably place yourself somewhere in between.

The graphs top out at 100 percent, but that's not meant to imply a limit to your potential. As the arrow indicates, if you feel you're more than 100 percent productive in an area, shade that in.

For example, if you are consistently devoting time and energy to your family, you might shade the family scale to 75 percent or higher. On the other hand, if you're currently devoting less than optimal time to family because of work demands, you might shade that area only to 25 percent or less. The goal is to assess where you are today in each of these areas.

ASSESSING YOUR PERSONAL LIFE

Do you regularly take time to enjoy and nurture your family? Or do you let other priorities usurp family time so that you occasionally feel unbalanced, unfulfilled, and even guilty?

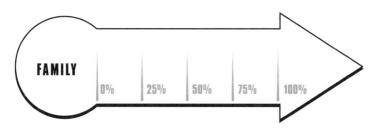

Does your career add excitement, satisfaction, and accomplishment to your life? Or does it tend to drain your energy, cause you to feel frustrated, and pull you away from other important desires and goals?

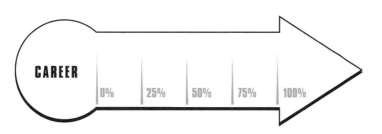

Do you manage your money well, so that you have financial freedom to pursue your life's goals and prepare for retirement? Or are you plagued by financial worries and debts?

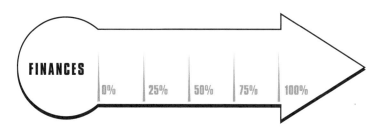

Do you care for your body through regular exercise, a good diet, and other healthful habits, so that you can pursue your goals with physical energy and stamina? Or do you neglect activities that promote good health and operate with less than optimal energy, mental alertness, and pleasure?

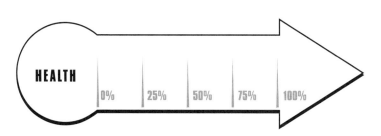

Do you regularly seek to develop your mind and increase your enjoyment of life by reading good books and exposing yourself to new ideas? Or do you allow the pressures of life to keep you from expanding your knowledge and awareness?

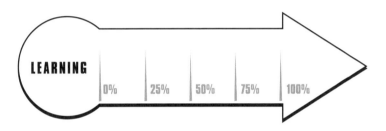

Do your values and beliefs provide a supportive foundation that gives meaning, purpose, and direction to your life? Or do you sometimes have difficulty establishing priorities, making decisions, and finding fulfillment because you haven't clearly identified your values and purpose?

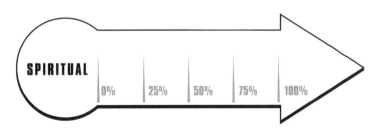

Do you frequently enjoy pleasurable and relaxing occasions with friends and acquaintances? Or do other priorities severely limit your vacations and times of recreation?

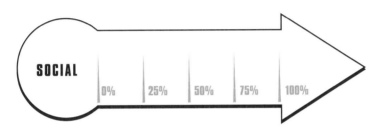

Do you regularly take advantage of opportunities to serve your community and establish new relationships by working on worthwhile causes? Or do other activities limit your ability to perform civic service?

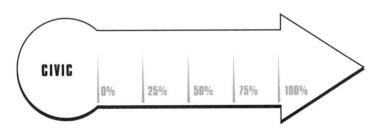

ASSESSING YOUR PROFESSIONAL LIFE

Is your career aligned with your passion, so that your professional activities are dynamic, exciting, and fulfilling expressions of who you really are? Or does your work often seem tedious, boring, and meaningless?

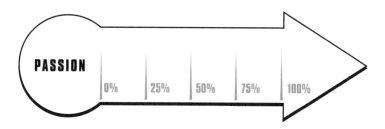

Do you have a clear vision that imbues your professional life with purpose and energy? Or do you primarily concentrate on short-term challenges that fail to give you a sense of purpose and satisfaction?

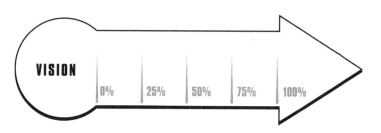

Do you have goals for your professional life that provide motivation and direction? Or do your day-to-day activities often seem scattered and unfocused?

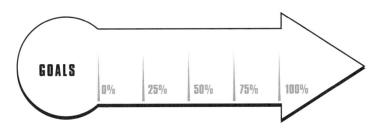

Do you manage your time and your activities effectively, so that your efforts generally produce significant, positive results? Or do you often find yourself wasting time and accomplishing less than you desire?

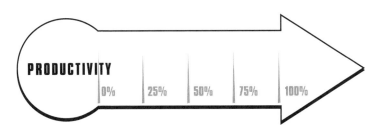

Are you skilled in communicating with different types of people, so that you experience success in building relationships, presenting ideas, and establishing connections? Or are you insecure and fearful about developing new relationships and selling yourself and your ideas?

COMMUNICATIONS 0% 25% 50% 75% 100%

Do you have a positive attitude that empowers you to surmount obstacles and accomplish your goals? Or do you often feel discouraged and victimized?

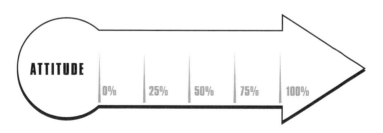

ATTITUDE 0% 25% 50% 75% 100%

Have you built an accountability structure that gives you accurate assessments of your progress, so that you maximize your success and guard against failure? Or do you navigate through your career with little feedback and support from others?

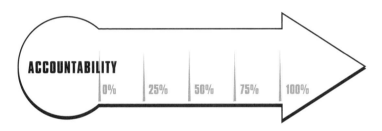

Are you continually acquiring new knowledge and skills through education, training, and self-improvement, so that you are able to rapidly progress to greater levels of responsibility? Or are you stagnated at some past level of mental ability and skill proficiency?

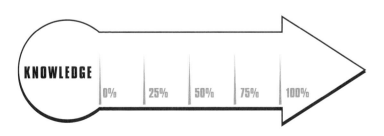

Now that you've shaded in your responses on both the personal and professional graphs, take a few minutes to look over your answers. Are you surprised by what you see? Note below the areas of your life where you want to focus more attention. Any areas where you score below 50 percent deserve consideration.

EXERCISE # 2

- **Answer the questions below to gain more clarity about where you are today:**

  ⊙ In what areas of your life do you feel stuck?

  ⊙ If you could change one thing about your personal life, what would it be?

  ⊙ If you could change one thing about your professional life, what would it be?

The skills below are important for professional success. Check the ones you currently possess. Circle the ones you would most like to develop. List any other skills you would like to add.

☐ Selling & Influencing

☐ Presenting Ideas

☐ Communicating Orally

☐ Communicating in Writing

☐ Networking

☐ Managing People

☐ Managing Time

☐ Managing Paperwork & Projects

☐ Leading

☐ Creating

☐ Strategizing

☐ Using Technology

☐ _____

☐ _____

Review your answers. How long have you felt the same way? Consistency can be one indication of reliability. Consider keeping a journal in the back of this book. Refer to your journal periodically to gauge how your observations stand the test of time.

ADDITIONAL EXERCISES

You're no doubt in a hurry to get in the race, but don't rush this evaluation process. Before you move ahead, it's important to know where you are. A good start is essential to a successful race. Appendix II lists some additional resources that can help you identify your starting line.

YOU'RE OFF AND RUNNING!

Have you done enough thinking to identify your starting point? Have you pinpointed the areas you want to change? Then congratulations! You are ready to begin running the race.

No matter what your level of ability, you have more potential than you can ever develop in a lifetime.

ANONYMOUS

Chapter Three:

You Can Do It!

hen I introduced you to Ralph in Chapter 1,
he was earning more than $200,000 a year as
a manger. Although he was bored with his job, he
was unable to break free from the seductive snare of
perceived financial security.

No job is secure enough, no salary is large
enough, if you're not living your passion. When
people try to hold on to jobs they don't like for the

sake of perceived security, a variety of "unfortunate events" may occur.

Maybe they don't perform at their best, and they find themselves demoted or even fired. Perhaps their unhappiness spills over into their relationships and poisons their family life. Or possibly living without excitement and purpose causes them to become addicted to harmful behaviors.

On the other hand, people who pursue their passions usually attain both success and fulfillment. Yes, they may have to take risks, and that can be scary. But in life, we either risk or rust. Reaching for goals beyond our immediate grasp summons our courage and energizes our purpose. Pursuing our passion ennobles our lives.

The money may not be there at first. Sometimes we need to let go of money to grab hold of passion. If you pursue your vision, I firmly believe that the money will follow. In the long run, you may actually earn much more than before. But even if you don't, the other benefits of living your passion – a sense of purpose, success, joy, fulfillment, and accomplishment – will more than make up the difference.

STEP ONE

The most important step toward your goals is the first step. It's also often the hardest step.

No doubt you're familiar with Michelangelo's beautiful sculpture of David. In Irving Stone's highly acclaimed book *The Agony and the Ecstasy,* Michelangelo struggles to decide how he will depict David as a hero. Up to that time, most artists had portrayed the heroic David standing over the slain Goliath. But as Michelangelo thought about it, he realized that wasn't David's most heroic moment. David's most heroic moment was when he picked up the first stone.

Ralph isn't out of the trap yet; he's still at his same job. But he's taken an important step forward. He recognizes that he must make a change if he wants to make his life count. He has picked up the first stone.

How about you? Do you recognize the need for change in your life? Maybe you don't need to change your job, but you do need to change your attitude, or your priorities, or your vision of where you want to be. If you're stuck in any area of your life, the first step is to decide whether you're ready to change.

TAKING CHARGE

In Chapter 1 you also met Teresa, who was frustrated because her boss didn't have a plan for the business and she didn't have a plan for her life. Teresa quit her job and hired me as her coach. Understandably she was insecure and fearful about what the future might hold.

As we worked together over a period of time, she decided to focus on her passion, which is interior design. For years she had put this passion on the back burner, even though she already had some good experience and education in the field. Now she wanted to move ahead, but she lacked confidence. She hesitated because she didn't recognize how truly talented she was.

In order for people to change, they must take 100 percent responsibility for deciding what they want out of life. And they must take 100 percent responsibility for recognizing that they have the ability to achieve their goals. After two months, Teresa took the first step: she clarified what she wanted. Over the next year she realized that she had the capability to attain it.

Today Teresa runs her own successful interior design business. To top it off, two investors recently approached her about starting a business to design and build million-dollar homes. Even now, as I write her story, they are developing plans that promise to open up exciting new opportunities for her.

In her previous job, Teresa's boss was primarily interested in activity, so she tried to keep busy. Now she's much better than busy; she's productive, and she feels a sense of accomplishment.

You'll be excited when you hear what happened to George, the man I introduced you to in Chapter 1. As you may recall, the sudden death of one of his two partners forced him to take over the management of his food products company. But George didn't know what to do. He felt overwhelmed and paralyzed.

George and his surviving partner asked me to coach them as they developed a plan for the business. With a roadmap in hand, their anxieties subsided and they focused 100 percent of their energies on executing the plan. They also wisely took steps to fill some gaps in their business. For example, they hired a bookkeeper and engaged the services of a marketing firm.

As a result, the company's revenues have doubled annually for the past three years. The business is regularly adding new product lines and new customers. At some future point, George and his partner will probably bring in a chief operating officer to oversee day-to-day operations.

George did not stay stuck, and he did not give in to fear. He took responsibility for the business and made it successful. If George and his partner can develop a plan and achieve their goals, you can too.

IT'S NOT TOO LATE

Let's get an update on another client from Chapter 1. When we last visited with Roger, he was a frustrated sixty-year-old president of a financial services firm who was considering retirement.

Instead of retiring, Roger and I began working together. I assisted him and his staff as they developed a business plan and set goals aligned with their plan. Instead of waiting for business to come to them, they identified markets with the greatest potential, hired the right people to serve those markets, and actively pursued new business.

Since Roger picked up that first stone and said, "Yes, I can do it! I want to change," his business has increased more than 30 percent each year. He became proactive rather than reactive. He's excited about his firm's direction and is no longer thinking about retirement.

Roger's encouraging story should remind us of this important truth: no matter how old you are, you still have time to change. Life is a marathon, not a sprint. It's a journey, not a stroll.

You may need to change the way you perform your job, like Roger. If so, some of the resources listed in Appendix II will be helpful to you.

You may need to change your attitudes and priorities. We'll address those subjects later in this book, especially in Chapters 8 and 9.

Perhaps you'll even need to change your career. Just because you've always been a lawyer, or an accountant, or a pharmacist doesn't mean you always have to be one.

At any age you have the ability to "reinvent" yourself so that you can pursue your passion and your vision. Are you aimlessly drifting back and forth across an expansive sea of unfulfilled possibilities and unrealized dreams? You still have time to get back on course and seize the opportunities that lie before you. You're never too old to change!

Author Carl Bard wisely said, "Though no one can go back and make a brand new start, anyone can start from now and make a brand new ending."

A BIG HURDLE

Are you ready to start improving your life? Are you excited about taking responsibility for creating your future? If you feel a bit hesitant, there may be one more hurdle you need to overcome: fear.

Change is almost always frightening. Virtually all of us need to face our fears before we can move forward.

Jim was very happy and successful as a sales manager for a medical supply company, but the extensive travel was wearing him down. So he accepted a similar job with another firm. There was just one problem. His new boss now did what he used to do. Jim's title was the same, but his responsibilities were less.

When Jim first engaged my services as his coach, he was bored, unhappy, and undecided about which way to go. He and his wife had a nice home and some cash reserves that were underutilized, so they agreed to focus first on improving their personal financial situation. As they gained skills and confidence, they bought two rental properties and hired a financial advisor.

Then we turned our attention to Jim's career. "I could transfer to another job within the same company," he told me, "but what I'd most love to do is start my own business."

Jim's idea was to provide a new kind of service within the medical supply industry that promised to save his customers considerable time and money. The concept seemed sound and the potential seemed large. I asked him if he planned to do it.

"I'm afraid," he admitted. "I don't think I'm brave enough."

Fear of failure keeps multitudes of people stuck in the starting blocks. But as psychologist and television personality Dr. Joyce Brothers said, "The person interested in success has to learn to view failure as a healthy, inevitable part of the process of getting to the top."

Abraham Maslow, the well-known psychologist, said, "One can choose to go back toward safety or forward toward growth. Growth must be chosen again and again; fear must be overcome again and again."

Right now Jim is writing his business plan. When he finishes, he'll have a pretty good idea whether he wants to pursue his vision. I don't know how this will turn out. But the process of expressing his vision has caused him to see that he is ready for a change. He recently told me, "I realize that where I am today is not where I want to be."

GET READY

Are you ready for a change? Recognizing that you're stuck is the first step forward.

I hope you are encouraged by these true stories of some of my clients who have recognized the need for change, confronted their fears, and moved forward. They have transitioned from "stuck in the starting blocks" to "running the race to win." If they can do it, so can you!

In subsequent chapters, you'll be exposed to information and exercises that will help you clarify your dreams and direction. You'll discover how to create a vision of where you want to be. You'll learn about the three critical success factors of passion, attitude, and communication. And you'll find out how to develop the plans and take the actions to propel you across the finish line you set for yourself.

The secret of getting ahead is getting started.
SALLY BERGER

SET

Chapter Four:

What's Your Passion?

I want to tell you about a businessman I know named Steve. After graduating from college, he became a successful accountant, with offices in three locations. One day, as he caught himself watching the clock, he realized what time it was. It was time to make a change.

At age thirty-three, Steve sold his accounting business and launched out in a whole new direction.

He had always loved restaurants, so he started one. Today he owns twelve. They're all very popular, and they all display his creative flare. For example, some resemble authentic Irish pubs. Walk through the door and you feel as if you've been transported to the Emerald Isle. Others are oyster bars decorated with heavy oak and copper lanterns, just like something you'd find in the historic district of Boston.

Recently I attended a leadership event for the high school youth in our community. On this particular day the subject was entrepreneurship. The forty-five teenagers sat in rapt attention as Steve told them about his background, his choices, and his successful business.

As Steve concluded his presentation, a young fellow said to him, "In my eyes, you're a real hero. How did you accomplish all that?"

"When I was young," Steve replied, "my mom used to have lots of dreams. She'd tell me about them, but she never acted on them. I decided I wouldn't make that same mistake. I've acted on my dreams."

Then Steve asked the student, "What do you want to do with your life?"

"I want to be a pianist," he answered, "but

my parents say I won't earn enough money doing that."

Will this young man pursue his dream to be a pianist? It will be an uphill battle, unless he receives encouragement along the way.

DREAMS AND TREASURES

Do you have any friends and acquaintances who are not living their dreams because others have discouraged them. Do you know any who are living their parents' dreams instead of their own? I know lots of people who are stuck in this trap. Maybe it's snared you, too.

One of my friends is a pharmacist because his father was a pharmacist and his grandfather was a pharmacist. Sadly, he has no passion for what he spends most of his waking hours doing. And up to this point he's been unable to admit to himself that he watches the clock.

Passion is "an ardent affection or strong devotion to a person, object, or purpose." Passion is characterized by boundless enthusiasm, zeal, drive, and intense feelings of desire. Passion evokes confidence, positive attitudes, and energy. When one approaches life with passion, obstacles tend to diminish and accomplishments begin to flourish.

I firmly believe that passion is the most important component of success. Of the many treasures that lie within you, passion is your crown jewel. People live happier, more productive lives when their goals and actions are aligned with their passion.

It's unfortunate when passion gets trampled under foot. Usually the people who dampen our dreams mean well. Sometimes our dreams really are "pipe dreams," and we need to know the truth. Not every kid who wants to be a professional athlete is going to make it.

But usually it's better to allow the dreams to bubble to the surface, so they can float through the air for a while as they're tested by time. Many will "pop" and ultimately disappear, and that's fine. Maybe there's another more worthwhile dream underneath that can't come up until the first one's out of the way.

Dreaming ignites passion. Passion fuels success.

AH-HA!

Have you suppressed your passion? Maybe you didn't think your dreams were "practical" or "professional" or "prestigious" enough. Perhaps your parents or other significant influences in your life discouraged you from following your heart's desires. Possibly you've been living to please others more than yourself.

It's never too late to change. The first step forward is to acknowledge where you are. If you've been watching the clock while the precious days of your life tick by, summon the courage to admit it.

Nothing gives me greater joy than helping people gain valuable new insights that improve their lives. I call these revelatory occasions "Ah-HA!" moments. Discovering your passion is the ultimate "Ah-HA!"

In the remainder of this chapter you will find tools and exercises to help you dig down deep, so you can experience the joy of saying, "Ah-HA! That's what I want to do! That's what's really important to me!"

But first a word of caution: discovering passion often isn't quick or easy, especially if it's deeply buried. You might have to excavate through some bedrock before uncovering your heart's desire.

TREASURE HUNTING

Take your time and don't be afraid to experiment. Be willing to dig "dry holes" before you find the treasure.

To get your juices flowing, I'm going to give you three definitions of passion and ask you to answer some related questions:

1. A passion is something you love so much that you will always make time for it.

It gives you such joy that you're happy to stop what you're doing, rearrange your calendar, change your priorities, and postpone other activities so you can engage in it.

Ask yourself:

⊙ What are the things in my life that I already make time for?

⊙ What would I like to spend more time doing?

⊙ What am I able to focus on so intently that I tune out other distractions?

⊙ What do I usually do promptly and well, so I don't have to make excuses?

⊙ What activities give me the most joy?

2. A passion is something you love so much that you are willing to invest time, energy, and money in the pursuit of being the best you can be.

Mediocrity is not an option. Excellence is the only acceptable standard. You are willing to expend the effort to perfect your skills, always striving to be more proficient today than you were yesterday. Your commitment to perfect your knowledge and ability in this area is ongoing – it has no finish line.

Ask yourself:

⊙ What things in my life do I already approach with a consuming desire to be the best I can be?

⊙ What types of people do I seek out to learn from?

⊙ What am I willing to spend money on to improve my knowledge and abilities?

⊙ What do I get most excited conversing about?

⊙ What would I most like to become an expert on so I can tell others about it, possibly even by lecturing and writing books?

3. **A passion is something you love so much that you feel a great pain when you don't or can't do it.**

When you don't make time for your passion, you may feel a bit empty. Life is less exciting. A nagging feeling tells you that you've been slacking off or emphasizing the wrong priorities.

Ask yourself:

⊙   What are the things in my life that I must do, or else I will feel a sense of loss?

⊙   If I imagine myself looking back from the end of my life, what would I most regret not doing?

⊙   What makes me most angry, frustrated, or upset when I can't do it to my full potential?

WHAT'S REALLY IMPORTANT?

Reflect on the answers you have given thus far. Then, take a few minutes and list some activities and priorities that are important to you.

1. List those things that you make time for.

2. List those areas where you want to excel.

3. List those things that you regret not having time to do.

If you are unclear about your passion at this point, I suggest that you utilize some of the resources I've recommended in Appendix II. Don't try to rush this important step. Take time to identify your passion before moving on. Use the journal to record your thoughts.

SOME ENCOURAGING STORIES

As we close this chapter, I want to encourage you with some true stories of people who are living lives that are aligned with their passions. I hope they assist you in discovering your own "Ah-HA!"

Mark enjoyed his job at a national communications company and was looking forward to a long career. When management suddenly laid him off during a downsizing, he was devastated.

He drove home in despair. But by the time he arrived at his front door, he had decided it was time to follow his passion. He would pursue a career as a motivational speaker and writer.

In the last three years, Mark has written five books, become a well-paid speaker with the National Speakers Bureau, and developed a lucrative consulting business. Because he is living his passion, he is more successful personally and professionally than ever before.

* * *

Pat faced an uphill battle when he took over as the new football coach at our local high school. The year before, the team had won one game and lost nine. But Pat was passionate and confident. The players caught his enthusiasm. They lifted weights, ran, and practiced with dedication. Their record improved that first year: they won half their games.

During the off-season the confidence and excitement continued to grow. The freshmen, sophomores, and juniors worked out and attended summer football camp. That fall, twice as many guys reported for the first practice. Most were in outstanding shape.

The stands were almost full for the first

game of the season. The team won that game, and the next. In the third game, they faced an opponent who had defeated them the previous year by a score of 40 to 0.

Before a packed house, the team played their hearts out – and won! The student body charged the field in celebration. No one in the stands will ever forget that evening.

Under Pat's leadership, the team went all the way to the district finals. They lost, but they didn't get discouraged. The players resolved to do even better next year. Why? Because Pat's passion is contagious. He elevated their vision and ignited their desire.

* * *

April is a successful engineer, but her passion is making specialty cakes. She is thrilled when people rave about her cakes, and she enjoys improving her baking skills through on-going training. The thought of not pursuing this vision makes her miserable.

When I first met April, she vividly

described to me her vision about how she wants her future storefront to look. I've enjoyed watching her build up her cake business on a part-time basis while she wisely continues her engineering career. At some point she plans to leave engineering and fully commit to the career she's most passionate about.

+ ✳ +

Think of some people you've read about who have achieved significant things. Do names like Martin Luther King Jr., Mother Teresa, Bill Gates, Tiger Woods, and Walt Disney come to mind? Now, think of some people of accomplishment you know personally, even though they're not famous. What are they like? I am certain that one common thread runs through all of their lives, and that is passion.

PURSUE YOUR PASSION

I hope I've convinced you to pursue your passion. And I hope the tools provided in this book will get you off to a good start. But remember, discovering your passion is a life-long process.

Your passion can evolve over time, so never stop searching for that crown jewel of treasures that lie within you.

You can't pursue your passion unless you can visualize it. If you don't have a clear picture of what you want, your passion will remain a vague, unrealizable dream.

We'll address the importance of visualizing your dreams in Chapter 6. But first, let's talk about the importance of knowing yourself.

"Don't ask yourself what the world needs - ask yourself what makes you come alive, and then go do it. Because what the world needs is people who have come alive."

HAROLD THURMAN WHITMAN

Chapter five:

Are You In Shape?

Before you can run a race, you need to get in shape. What kind of shape are you in now? What shape do you need to be in to win?

People come in all sorts of shapes. You have a specific shape, too. In this chapter, I want to help you take a fresh look at a few of the attributes that describe "you."

Why? Because when you're aware of your

strengths and weaknesses, you can plan your race to capitalize on the former and compensate for the latter. Just as an athlete trains for the contest, you can design your training regimen to develop the attitudes and skills that you will need to achieve your goals.

Let's first focus on the positive. Take a moment and write down on the journal pages in the back of this book some of the positive behaviors and attributes that define you. What do others praise about you? What qualities are you most proud of?

When you are ready, look back over your list. Some of your attributes are pretty impressive, aren't they! But I didn't give you this exercise to puff you up. I wanted you to get a better idea of your strengths and interests so you can leverage them.

Not everyone has all your strengths. If fact, no one does. You have a unique set of gifts that you can use to serve others. Usually you will make the biggest contributions and have the greatest probability of success when you serve from your strengths.

Now list some of your weaker attributes that threaten to hold you back or trip you up. Decide which ones you want to work on. Don't plan to devote as much time to shoring up your weaknesses as you devote to developing your strengths. But awareness of your weaker attributes will allow you to strengthen and compensate for the ones that might cause you problems.

FOUR KEY ATTRIBUTES

For the remainder of this chapter, we're going to focus on four key attributes that significantly affect success. As you examine these attributes, take an honest inventory to see where you stand. Then work on areas you want to improve.

The attributes we'll discuss are *Focus, Commitment, Awareness,* and *Perseverance.* Of course, that's not an exhaustive list. But I've noticed in working with many people that these attributes have tremendous power to either promote or hinder success.

FOCUS

You've heard the expression, "Keep your eye on the ball." Many people don't succeed because they get distracted from their goals; they lose focus.

Identifying your goals is essential, but not sufficient. You must *pursue* your goals with focus and discipline.

One way people lose focus is by failing to draw clear lines between their professional and personal lives. Many people who are self-employed struggle with this issue, especially if they work out of their homes.

Roger, the sixty-year-old president of a financial services firm whom we met in Chapter 1, confuses his personal life and his professional life in a different way. One of his biggest strengths is also one of his greatest weaknesses: he's extremely compassionate. As a result, he sometimes hires people based on his personal compassion for *their* needs rather than on his professional judgment of his *company's* needs.

Because he sometimes hires people who don't fit, his employees too often under-perform. By trying to "help" his employees, he frequently "enables" their own counterproductive behaviors. In the end, he doesn't help himself or them.

Roger's business is doing well, but it could be doing even better. Roger acknowledges that he needs more discipline and focus. He realizes that he must more clearly distinguish between what satisfies his personal needs and what serves his professional goals. It's too early to tell if he will change, but his awareness of his weakness is an important first step.

Focused people are disciplined. They do the most important things first. Undisciplined people tend to tackle enjoyable tasks first and postpone less pleasant tasks, regardless of their importance.

Business owners and entrepreneurs who work for themselves are particularly vulnerable to this temptation. That's why they desperately need to set up an accountability structure. We'll talk more about accountability in Chapter 12.

Another of my clients decided to change direction and launch out on a new career. But he seems to have lost focus. He doesn't set aside adequate time to research potential jobs because he's single and he's too busy enjoying his social life. His need for personal companionship is distracting him from accomplishing his professional goals.

As a coach, my goal is to help people see where they want to be and support them as they develop their plans, set their goals, and take the necessary steps to move forward. Will this client ever free himself from this counter-productive behavioral trap? Only if he decides to take responsibility for his life and focus on his goals.

Beware of traps that can rob your life of focus. Some people don't live focused lives because they've suppressed their passions, as we've discussed in Chapter 4. Other people try so hard to fit in and please that they fail to nourish their own unique potential. They're afraid to take the types of risks that must precede virtually all productive change.

When purpose doesn't drive us toward accomplishment, conformity pulls us toward mediocrity. "People pleasers" accomplish very little of significance.

Focus originates from within. Anna Quindlen astutely said, "The thing that is really hard, and really amazing, is giving up on being perfect and beginning to work on becoming yourself."

Are you living a focused life?

COMMITMENT

Commitment always precedes accomplishment. Commitment is a subjective, foundational quality that pervades all of life. Its presence or absence is often betrayed by seemingly inconsequential actions.

Do you know people who promise to do something but fail to follow through? "I'll call you tomorrow," they say, but don't. "I'll have this job done by next Thursday," but it's not. "I'll meet you at 5:00 p.m.," but they habitually show up fifteen minutes late.

As the saying goes, those are not the people you want to share a foxhole with. Trustworthiness is built on keeping commitments. Keeping commitments is evidence of respect for others.

Committed people take responsibility for their lives and their actions. They don't make excuses and shift blame. They're coachable because they acknowledge their mistakes and learn. You can count on their word. They earn people's trust and confidence and almost always go farther in life.

How about you? Do you keep your word? Do you take responsibility for your actions and your life?

Are you a person of commitment?

AWARENESS

You will be more successful when you are aware of yourself and others.

We've already touched on the importance of knowing yourself. That's what this chapter – indeed, this whole book – is about. When you know yourself, you can align your goals with your passion, harness your strengths, and guard against your weaknesses to ensure maximum success.

Part of knowing yourself is to understand what type of professional environment best suits your values and temperament. I coach numerous clients who are having problems at work. Most of them can do the job, but the culture is wrong; they don't fit in.

One of my current clients thrives on encouragement, but her boss tears people down more than he builds them up. Whenever employees in her office do something worth celebrating, he fails to praise them and instead points out something else they need to do better. More often than not, he blames others when things go wrong instead of taking responsibility for his own failings.

To make matters worse, she wants and needs direction, but her boss doesn't plan. He's reactive rather than proactive. Because the environment is wrong for her, she's withering on the vine.

I advise my clients to check out companies thoroughly before accepting job offers. Talk to other employees and find out about the culture. How much structure exists? Is there a plan? How much pressure? What are the values? How are decisions made? Is there freedom to perform, or does management exercise excessive control? After you assess the company, take a self-inventory of your needs to make sure it's a fit.

In addition to knowing yourself, you need to be aware of others. You'll be a more successful sales person if you are alert to the needs of others - their fondest desires and deepest pains. You'll have a more successful career in any field if you're keenly aware of your boss's priorities and your company's goals. You'll be a better communicator if you know how your audience prefers to listen. (We'll talk more about communications in Chapter 10.)

To increase your success, become aware of your strengths, weaknesses, desires, and needs, while at the same time discerning the strengths, weaknesses, desires, and needs of others.

Are you aware?

PERSEVERANCE

Some runners take eight hours or more to complete a marathon. But when they finally do cross the finish line, the crowd cheers. People respect their perseverance.

I've noticed four types of runners in the race of life.

The first group of runners may start out fast. But when they encounter obstacles and challenges, they slow down or quit. They forget that life is a marathon and not a sprint. They don't persevere.

Other runners appear to have perseverance, but they lack imagination and initiative. They just plow ahead as if in a trance, without trying anything new. Maybe they'll finish one of these days, and that's better than quitting. But they usually don't accomplish as much as they could.

Still others change course too readily when they encounter obstacles. Rather than persevering, they lose sight of their original goals and head off in completely different directions.

Successful runners who persevere wisely comprise the fourth group. When they meet challenges, they evaluate the situation, revise their plans, and pursue their goals using a new approach.

This last group is not surprised or discouraged by difficulties. They expect to encounter obstacles in the pursuit of worthwhile goals. They would agree with Frank A. Clark, who said, "If you find a path with no obstacles, it probably doesn't lead anywhere."

I've had clients tell me, "I want to start my own business, but what if it doesn't work?" That statement indicates the absence of perseverance and the presence of fear. Fear is one of the biggest enemies you will encounter on your way to the finish line. Fear of failure, fear of rejection, fear of ridicule, fear of change – they all seek to undermine your perseverance.

> "I've missed over nine thousand shots in my career," said Michael Jordan, the retired professional basketball player. "I've lost almost three hundred games. Twenty-six times I've been trusted to take the game-winning-shot...and missed. I've failed over and over and over again in my life. And that is why I succeed."

Perseverance is strengthened by the pursuit

of goals aligned with passion. When your eyes are focused on meaningful goals that you are passionate about, you will see obstacles only with your peripheral vision. Perseverance will drive you over them or guide you around them.

"Most of our obstacles would melt away if, instead of cowering before them, we should make up our minds to walk boldly through them," said Orison Swett Marden, the founder of *Success Magazine.*

Successful accomplishment builds confidence and overcomes worry. When you look back from your achievements, the challenges that at the outset loomed large will seem strangely diminished. "If you want to test your memory," says E. Joseph Cossman, "try to remember what you were worrying about a year ago today."

Lucille Ball, the late comic actress, said, "One of the things I learned the hard way was that it doesn't pay to get discouraged. Keeping busy and making optimism a way of life can restore your faith in yourself."

When you look back from an even greater distance, obstacles that once seemed like enemies have a way of turning into friends. "A man's greatest strength develops at the point where he overcomes his greatest weakness," said Elmer G. Letterman.

Are you ready to persevere all the way to the finish line?

HONESTY

As we close this chapter, permit me to add one more important quality to the list: honesty. When you step back and take an honest look at your strengths and weaknesses, you increase your probability of success.

Recognize and appreciate your strengths so you can capitalize on them. Acknowledge the areas where you want and need to grow, so you can develop them and compensate for them.

Personal growth starts with an honest appraisal. What kind of shape are you in? Find out, and design your training regimen. Give priority to developing the attributes that are most essential to success, such as focus, commitment, awareness, and perseverance.

It is not the mountain we conquer, but ourselves.
SIR EDMUND HILLARY

Chapter Six

Where's The Finish Line?

efore you begin the race, you must know where the finish line is. You can be the fastest runner in the world and not win, if you run off in the wrong direction.

You also need benchmarks along the way to help you pace your race. Marathoners don't run simply by "feel." They know the times at which they want to reach every mile-marker.

In life you need a clear vision of where you're heading before you get going. And you need objectives and goals to serve as your mile-markers.

When we talk about vision in this chapter, I don't mean your really long-term finish line – what you're ultimately living for. Yes, that's extremely important. You need to be clear about your life's purpose and align your shorter-term vision and goals with it.

But in this book we're going to focus on where you want to be three to five years from now. Your vision is your finish line. Although you'll need to adjust your objectives, goals, and action steps to meet changing circumstances, your vision will remain constant until you accomplish it and refocus on another.

FORMULATING YOUR VISION

Imagine that you are standing on the shoreline, looking at an island on which your vision is a reality. Let's name this delightful piece of real estate "Ah-HA Island." Make the environment whatever you want – urban or rural, very active or rather quiet, modern or rustic, and so on.

Below are four questions to answer about that island. As you think about your answers, write them down. That will make them more real to you, and it will help raise other thoughts to your awareness.

Revisit your answers periodically during the next several days and add any new ideas that come to your mind. Gradually your vision will come into sharper focus.

1. Where do you want to be?

Describe what you want your life on Ah-HA Island to look like in three to five years. If you desire a better relationship with your spouse or kids, capture that vision in writing. If your vision is to have a better job or take your business to a higher level, write down what that looks like. If it's both, write that down.

2. What would you like to see?

What would you like to see on Ah-HA Island once you get there? What kind of environment do you want? Whom do you want to have with you? What kind of resources do you want at your disposal?

3. What do you want to be doing?

What do you picture yourself doing? How do you picture yourself interacting with others? What are you creating, building, selling, thinking about, and so on?

4. How do you want to feel?

Exercise your imagination so your feelings come alive. Do you feel excited? Satisfied? Creative? Useful? Capture your emotions on paper. They will help you clarify your vision and possibly give birth to additional answers to the first three questions.

CLARIFYING YOUR VISION

Be creative; give yourself permission to dream and imagine. Think outside the box. Articulate your vision and insert yourself mentally into the imagined possibilities.

First and foremost, your vision should excite you. It should be so real that you can visualize it and emotionally "feel" it. If you can taste, touch, and smell it, that will give it even more power. The most effective vision evokes strong feelings, so that you're motivated every day to make it happen. To help you clarify your vision, ask yourself these three additional questions:

- ☉ If you were given an award in front of colleagues, family, and friends, what would you want to be recognized for?

- ☉ If you could be any person and be successfully engaged in any profession, who and what would you want to be and how would that look?

- ☉ What is your definition of an ideal life?

If you're struggling with this exercise, the culprit might be fear. Sometimes we have difficulty imagining the ideal future because we're afraid we'll fail to achieve it. To avoid the pain of disappointment, we sometimes suppress our dreams.

If you're in this situation, simply imagine yourself successful. Be encouraged by these words of Samuel Smiles: "Men who are resolved to find a way for themselves will always find opportunities enough; and if they do not find them, they will make them."

Initially, your vision may take you outside your comfort zone. But as you continue to think about it and imagine yourself operating within it, you will feel more comfortable moving toward it.

DESCRIBING YOUR VISION

When you are ready, put your vision in writing, drawing on the content of your answers above. To get you started, I've quoted below a few visions some of my clients created:

> "I'm a V.P. working in the financial services industry, enjoying the challenge of my job while mentoring others."

"I own a successful accounting firm providing services to wonderful clients, while providing career opportunities to my associates."

* * *

"I live every day with joy and happiness while providing financial security to my family."

* * *

"I live a life of balance every day."

* * *

You've probably noticed that the latter two visions, relating to the personal realm, happen to be much less specific than the first two. You might be wondering, are such general visions useful?

I can testify that both clients found them very helpful. For one, being joyful is a challenging and important goal that promises to significantly affect her success and fulfillment. She is very motivated to achieve it. The other client is an executive who told me, "I get excited looking forward to living a life of balance. I will know it when I get there."

Some individuals and organizations like to express their visions concretely; others prefer to be more open-ended. One of my business clients developed a very detailed vision that ideally suits its needs. Another client derives helpful guidance and motivation from its more general vision, "Quality flows through everything we do."

PURSUING YOUR VISION

Once you have the finish line in view, you can develop plans to take you there. You will need to specify objectives, goals, and action steps that are aligned with your vision. We'll talk about the important subjects of planning and goals in Chapters 7 and 8.

"The great successful men of the world have used their imagination…they think ahead and create their mental picture in all its details, filling in here, adding a little there, altering this a bit and that a bit, but steadily building…steadily building."

ROBERT COLLIER

PLAN

Chapter Seven:

Planning The Race

Successful runners plan their races. They have a strategy.

Successful people plan their professional and personal lives. They realize that failure to plan is planning to fail.

Planning is a prerequisite for success. That's why I've titled this book, *"Ready, Set, **Plan**, Go!"* If you don't plan before you go, you're certain to go somewhere you didn't plan.

Author and speaker Jim Rohn said, "I find it fascinating that most people plan their vacations with better care than they plan their lives. Perhaps that is because escape is easier than change."

Your interest in this book is evidence that you're willing to embrace change in order to succeed. Planning enables you to chart your course through change.

In this chapter we're going to talk about the importance of planning your professional and your personal life. You'll learn how to develop plans, identify objectives, set goals, and define the action steps you need to take to reach your goals. You might want to jot down key points that occur to you in the journal pages at the back of this book, so you can refer to them later.

VISION

As we discussed in Chapters 5 and 6, the planning process starts with your vision. Clarify your vision before you begin writing your professional and personal plans. Your plans should flow from and be aligned with your vision.

What does a successful personal life look like to you? Do you want healthy relationships with family and friends? Then get a clear picture of what that looks like. Where do you want to be professionally? Describe your vision in detail.

Successful people face all of the same challenges others face, but they don't get discouraged or quit. How do they do it? Most of them visualize their finish lines. They see in their minds what they want to become and achieve.

PLANS

Expert mountain climbers break their assault into a series of steps, carefully planning their path to the top. In the same way, you must plan how you will realize your vision.

You will want to develop two kinds of personal and professional plans:

- ⊙ Your **long-term** plans will deal with the bigger picture – where you want to be personally and professionally in three to five years.

- ⊙ Your **short-term** plans will describe what you intend to accomplish during the next year in order to move closer to accomplishing your long-term goals.

OBJECTIVES

List the objectives you want to accomplish in order to realize your vision. Specify what you want to achieve in the various major areas of your personal and professional life.

For example, if your vision entails making sure your children are well educated, an objective in your long-term plan might be to financially assist them in going to college. A short-term objective might be to set up college savings plans.

If part of your long-term professional plan is to expand your business, an objective in your long-term plan might be to open a satellite office. Objectives in your short-term plan might include conducting a feasibility study, picking a location, and arranging for additional capital.

GOALS

Next, set goals within your personal and professional plans that relate to each of your objectives.

For example, if one of your short-term personal objectives is to set up college savings plans for your children, a short-term goal might be to locate by a specific date a financial advisor who can help you.

If one of your short-term professional objectives is to introduce one new product during the next year, a supporting goal might be to complete a market research study by a specific date.

Set goals for all of the major areas of your personal life – family, career, finances, health, learning, spiritual, social, and civic – and for the major areas of your professional life. Write them down – that makes them more real – and put them where you can see them every day.

For each area of your life, organize your goals in order of priority. When you accomplish one goal, remove it from the list and celebrate. Elevate the next most important goal in that area of your life up to priority number one.

Often in the process of accomplishing your top goal in an area, you'll be pleasantly surprised to see yourself concurrently accomplishing other lower-priority goals.

Make sure your goals are "**WAY SMART.**" That means they should be –

- ⊙ **Written** – Writing down your goals makes them real and ensures that they are clear.

- ⊙ **Aligned** – Your goals should be aligned with your vision and with your plans so that they all work together in harmony.

- ⊙ **Yours** – Make your goals sincere. Some goals sound good, but if they don't reflect deeply felt desires, they have limited motivational value.

- ⊙ **Specific** – In order to provide clear direction and strong motivation, goals must be specific. Vague goals create confusion, frustration, and apathy.

- ⊙ **Measurable** – Measurable goals provide benchmarks for evaluating progress and performance. "Attain annual sales of $5 million" is a measurable business goal; "improve sales" is not. "Go out to dinner with spouse once a week" is a measurable personal goal; "spend more time with spouse" is not.

- ⊙ **Attainable** – Goals that are beyond reach produce frustration instead of motivation. For maximum accomplishment, set goals that are achievable.

- ⊙ **Realistically High** – Goals that are set too low can result in underachievement. Set realistically high goals that require innovation and dedication to accomplish.

- ⊙ **Time Bound** – Effective goals specify completion dates. The time component increases their usefulness for planning, decision-making, operational coordination, and evaluation. "Hire new sales manager" is a less effective business goal than "hire new sales manager by July 1."

ACTION STEPS

Most goals require action steps. For example, if a professional goal is to hire a new sales manager by July 1, immediate action steps might be to write a job description and contact a recruitment firm. If a personal goal is to set up college savings funds by July 1, action steps might be to call your banker for ideas, engage the services of a financial advisor, and buy a book on funding college educations.

When action steps require specific time commitments, put them on your calendar. For example, if you want to improve your health by exercising four times a week, schedule those workouts. If you want to develop a closer relationship with your family, make a commitment on your calendar to be home for dinner with the family a certain number of nights a week.

Translating actions steps into calendar appointments converts them from wishful thinking to practical doing. You probably won't find time to pursue activities you can't find time to schedule.

THE VALUE OF PLANNING

The process of planning forces you to think about your vision, objectives, goals, and action steps. Simply engaging in this process produces positive results, even before you begin implementing the plans.

Planning is not optional. It's a crucial ingredient for success, both personally and professionally. Goals elevate your decision-making. They serve as mile-markers to ensure that you take the right routes to arrive at the right place at the right time.

Author Og Mandino wisely said, "The victory of success is half won when one gains the habit of setting goals and achieving them. Even the most tedious chore will become endurable as you parade through each day convinced that every task, no matter how menial or boring, brings you closer to achieving your dreams."

Your plans are not straightjackets to constrain you. They're live documents intended to help you. Review them weekly or monthly, and revise and update them as necessary so they continue to be accurate and keep you on track.

For greater success, plan your work and work your plan!

"Please understand, my friend, that where you find yourself tomorrow is a function of the positive decisions and actions you take today."

AKIN A. AWOLAJA

Chapter Eight

Keeping Your Balance

H ave you ever seen a runner stumble and fall? Eric Liddell did that in the movie *Chariots of Fire*. To his credit, he picked himself up and won the race. But if you lose your balance in the race of life, you may not be able to recover so quickly.

You can have a wonderful professional plan, execute it to perfection, and not achieve satisfaction and success if your life's not in balance. You need to plan your personal life with as much care as your professional life. In fact, you may need to devote attention to areas of your personal life before you can effectively address your professional life.

LET'S GET PERSONAL

Helen sells artwork at galleries throughout the country. When she and I first met, her business was less than successful, so she asked me to be her coach.

In our initial meeting she shared some personal concerns. Perhaps because of her troubled marriage, she had neglected her health. She had lost confidence in herself, and concerns about her three sons were emotionally draining her.

We agreed to address her personal issues before tackling the business. Over the next several months she made some important changes to reorder her personal life. Now, as her health and other issues continue to improve, she's focusing attention on her business, which is beginning to take off.

"Success is the continual achievement of your own predetermined goals, stabilized by balance and purified by belief."[1] Notice that this defini-

---

1   Definition supplied by Resource Associates Corporation, 31 Hickory Road, Mohnton, PA 19540

tion doesn't mention money, but it does mention balance.

You cannot be fully successful professionally if you are not successful personally. You may have a great business plan, and it can be working to perfection. But you will only feel – and be – truly successful when you have *balance* and *synergy* in your life.

Balancing your professional and personal lives produces synergy. The resulting whole is greater than the sum of the parts. When your personal goals and professional goals are aligned, you will experience maximum growth, success, and satisfaction.

Examine your personal and professional goals to identify areas in which they might be in conflict. Adjust your priorities and revise your goals as necessary to make them mutually compatible and complementary.

For example, if one of your professional goals is to achieve 35 percent growth in your company's revenues in the next year, and one of your personal goals is to learn to play golf, think through how you will accomplish both. Be honest with yourself. If you feel tense or uncertain just thinking about how you will find time to do it, these goals are probably in conflict. Adjust your priorities to achieve better balance.

LET'S BE REALISTIC

You will never be able to totally balance your life. At some times your professional goals will demand so much attention that you'll have to defer working on some of your personal goals.

At other times events may occur – such as the birth of a child, a move to a new home, or a sickness in the family – that will force you to focus more attention on personal goals to the temporary detriment of your professional goals.

Although you should always strive for balance, you must be willing to embrace imbalance. Balance is not a static situation to be attained, but a dynamic goal to be pursued.

Balancing your personal and professional lives does not require "meshing" them. On the contrary, be alert so you don't allow one to unproductively encroach upon the other. For example, if you work at home, you will need to protect your time at the "office" by establishing well-defined boundaries that are understood by other family members.

How's your balance now? Are the various parts of your life integrated, or do you feel pulled a dozen directions, as if you're constantly rushing to and fro to keep all the balls in the air?

Are you relaxed enough to enjoy whatever you're doing at the moment, or do you often feel tense and guilty because you're not somewhere else? Do you make time for reading, thinking, and relaxing, or do you often feel overwhelmed by options, interruptions, and expectations?

Success involves more than money and career advancement. Success is holistic; it encompasses your whole life – personal and professional. Without balance, you will experience less success and fulfillment.

As you revise your goals to achieve your definition of balance, remember that your personal life is every bit as important as your professional life, perhaps more so.

I believe that being successful means having a balance of success stories across the many areas of your life. You can't truly be considered successful in your business life if your home life is in shambles.

ZIG ZIGLAR

GO!

Chapter Nine:

A Winning Attitude

Imagine talking with two runners before a race. One says, "I know I can win. I'm going to give it all I've got!" The other says, "I hope I'm not in over my head. Those other runners look pretty fit."

Who will run the better race? Undoubtedly the one with the more positive attitude!

Your attitude is the engine that drives you toward success – or failure. It forms the basis for your behaviors and for your perspective on life. Reggie Leach is right when he says, "Success is not the result of spontaneous combustion. You must set yourself on fire first."

Consider two people with the same sets of skills, knowledge, and experiences. But one has a positive attitude and the other a negative. Whom would you want to hire? Which one would you want to work for? What type of leader would you prefer to follow?

More people get fired because of poor attitudes and sloppy work habits than because of lack of skills and knowledge. Your attitude dramatically affects your success in every area or your life – career, family, personal relationships, community activities, and leisure enjoyment.

You must sustain a positive attitude in order to accomplish worthwhile goals. Positive attitudes produce positive behaviors that produce positive results. "We don't see things as they are," says Anais Nim, "we see them as we are." Your attitude toward life will determine life's attitude toward you.

YOUR ATTITUDE AFFECTS YOUR RELATIONSHIPS

Do you like to be around people with negative

attitudes? When you're in their presence, do you feel excited and happy, or lethargic and depressed? Do you have a desire to linger, or an urge to escape?

Attitudes are contagious. Other people catch yours. Depending on whether your attitude is positive or negative, they're either attracted to you or not. They either want to form a relationship with you or they want to avoid you.

A positive attitude is a key – perhaps the most important key – to building successful relationships. When you have a positive attitude, people are attracted to you like a magnet. I call it the "Attraction Factor."

"There is a basic law that like attracts like," observed author Norman Vincent Peale. "Negative thinking definitely attracts negative results. Conversely, if a person habitually thinks optimistically and hopefully, his positive thinking sets in motion creative forces – and success instead of eluding him flows toward him."

I've known and admired Laurie for many years. Like all of us, she faces difficulties in her life. But she's always positive, and she's constantly thinking of others. Several years ago when her friend's daughter was killed in an accident, she organized a memorial race. Over the years, money raised through those annual events has provided scholarships for high school students. Laurie sees opportunities for good even in tragedies.

Recently I asked Laurie how she stays so positive. She replied, "I just choose to look at life that way."

Attitude is a habit. If a negative attitude is holding you back, break that bad habit! Don't just keep repeating the same mistake over and over, expecting a different result. That's one definition of insanity!

No one is forcing you to be miserable. Misery is a choice. Why choose misery and failure when you can choose happiness and success? Why choose to be a victim when you can take control of your life?

Ralph Waldo Emerson rightly said, "As long as a man stands in his own way, everything seems to be in his way. Most of the shadows of life are caused by standing in our own sunshine."

LEARN TO BE POSITIVE!

Positive attitudes don't appear spontaneously. They're learned. You can learn like Laurie to see the glass half full. Learn to think positively!

Research has identified three different ways that we learn:

1. "Realization Moments" that occur when we suddenly realize something that we didn't understand before, such as a math concept or the solution to a problem. These experiences account for about 2 percent of our total learning.

2. "Impact Events" that reshape our perspectives and behaviors. The death of a loved one, the birth of a child, and shocking events such as September 11, 2001, are examples of Impact Events. These experiences account for another 2 percent of our learning.

3. "Repetitive Reinforcement" that enables us to gradually gain new knowledge through repetition over time. Through repetitive reinforcement we learn to tie our shoes, ride bikes, fly airplanes, and perform brain surgeries. In fact, we learn the multiplication tables, foreign languages, advanced calculus, and 96 percent of everything else we know through repetitive reinforcement!

You can learn to think positively by using the

same proven technique of repetitive reinforcement. Let's talk about four excellent ways you can utilize this powerful method: positive affirmations, positive resources, positive relationships, and positive focus.

POSITIVE AFFIRMATIONS

Positive affirmations are statements about what you want for yourself and what you want to become. For best results, I suggest that you make them *personal*, *positive*, and *present tense*.

For example, if you want to develop a healthier lifestyle, a suitable positive affirmation might be, "I am a person who lives a healthy lifestyle." If you would like to be more confident, you might affirm, "I am a person of high self-esteem."

Create positive affirmations that align with your goals in the various areas of your life. Write them down and recite them out loud at least three times a day – morning, noon, and night. If you're a visual person, consider portraying your affirmations with graphics, such as photos from magazines.

Whenever I present on this subject, I encourage the participants in the audience to give me a call in thirty days and let me know if they've become any of their affirmations. Recently someone who attended one of my presentations sent me the following e-mail:

> Hi Joan – It's been a month since I've been saying my affirmations, and I'm following your request and e-mailing back. They really have an amazing power! The hardest one for me is now coming off my list and being replaced with another. Thanks so much for your inspiration! Janet

POSITIVE RESOURCES

"Garbage in, garbage out," the computer professionals correctly say. The same is true for your mind.

To develop a positive attitude, read positive books and magazines. If you spend lots of time driving in your car, listen to positive books on tape. Every day we're bombarded by enough negative input to discourage even the most confirmed optimist, and we're often unaware of its debilitating effect. Watch what you ingest into your mind. Go on a positive diet!

You'll enjoy life more if you spend at least

twenty minutes a day reading good literature. Select books and magazines that will increase your knowledge and expand your breadth of awareness. Find encouraging articles that focus your mind on what you want to become. All types of reading materials – biographies, poetry, spiritual inspiration and edification, professional development, quality fiction, self-help – are healthy food for your mind if they grow you in positive ways.

POSITIVE RELATIONSHIPS

Often we don't realize how much we are affected by the negative influences around us. Just as we are warned that second-hand smoke can give us cancer, I want to warn you that hanging around pessimists can give you a negative attitude.

Avoid negative thinkers, unless your goal is to help them become more positive. Spend time with people who know who they are and where they're going.

Louise is a positive, upbeat person. During our coaching sessions we discussed her desire to get a new job. "But one of my friends always discourages me from making a change," she confided to me. "Every time I interview for a new job, she tells me it isn't right for me. As a matter of fact, she's negative about most everything in my life. After I spend time with her, I feel emotionally down."

Louise decided to limit the time she spent with her friend. Without the negative influence, she was better able to move forward with her life. She took a new job that suited her perfectly.

But a funny thing happened when Louise told her "friend" how happy she was in her new position. Her friend became noticeably cool. In fact, she essentially withdrew her friendship. Perhaps because Louise had moved forward in a positive direction, there was no longer enough negativity to sustain the relationship.

Some people feed on negativity. Avoid them, because their attitudes are infectious.

POSITIVE FOCUS

You can't always control what happens to you, but you *can* always control your responses. Successful people choose to think positively *and* act positively. They focus on their goals rather than on their circumstances.

"Part of being a champ is acting like a champ,"

said figure skater Nancy Kerrigan. "You have to learn how to win and not run away when you lose. Everyone has bad stretches and real successes. Either way, you have to be careful not to lose your confidence or get too confident."

Focus is a matter of discipline, and discipline is largely a matter of managing your time and your priorities. You must choose to make every moment count. In Appendix II I recommend some excellent books that will help you improve your life management skills and develop positive attitudes.

Peter F. Drucker, author of the classic management book *The Effective Executive,* and Stephen R. Covey, author of the best selling book *The Seven Habits of Highly Effective People,* both observe that one of the keys to success is to put first things first.

You can't avoid interruptions and distractions, but you can plan to minimize their effect. When your desk and your calendar are out of control, your life will feel out of control and your attitude will suffer. Decrease your stress and increase your productivity by setting up systems that enable you to promptly and efficiently manage your time and your paperwork.

When are you most productive? If you accomplish challenging tasks best in the morning, arrange your schedule accordingly. Organize your calendar and manage your time to protect your peak-productivity periods.

Two of my coaching clients are partners in a small firm. One is a "morning person." The other doesn't really get going until afternoon. Meaningful discussions in the morning didn't work for one, and late afternoon meetings didn't work for the other. Communication between them was poor; tensions in the office were high.

After some discussion, the partners agreed to schedule regular meetings at noon. Communication and productivity immediately improved. The atmosphere throughout the company became more positive and relaxed.

Because your personal and professional lives are invariably intertwined, you must often choose between two desirable alternatives. Disciplined professionals choose the alternative that is better aligned with their goals.

POSITIVE RESULTS

Winners don't have positive attitudes because they win; they win because they have positive attitudes. To accelerate your success, acquire a positive attitude.

Your ability to manage your life affects your attitude. You can't act like a winner when you feel like a victim.

Life management is largely a matter of focus and discipline. Organize your time and priorities so that you act instead of react. Then watch your life take off!

Your living is determined not so much by what life brings you as by the attitude you bring to life; not so much by what happens to you as by the way your mind looks at what happens.

LEWIS L. DUNNINGTON

Chapter Ten

Passing The Baton

In a relay race, the baton pass is critical. If one runner doesn't cleanly hand off the baton, and the other runner doesn't firmly grasp it, the race can be lost.

Our personal and professional success depends to a significant degree upon the effectiveness of our handoffs – our interactions – with others.

Communication is vital to effective interactions.

In order to be successful, we must learn to give and receive communication crisply and clearly. In fact, communication is so important that I consider it to be one of the three key success factors, right along with passion and attitude.

WHAT IS COMMUNICATION?

Communication is a two-way process of sharing thoughts, feelings, and emotions to achieve under-standing and action. All communication aims to prompt a behavioral response.

Communication is a two-way process. To be effective, the handoff – both the giving and receiving – must be clean and clear.

If a tree falls in the forest and no one hears it, is there any sound? I don't claim to know the answer to that popular riddle. But I do know the answer to this question: If someone says something and the other person doesn't respond, is there any commu-nication? The answer to that is no!

Notice that the above definition of communica-tion is not restricted to written and spoken words. In fact, studies show that 55 percent of our commu-nications are non-verbal. They're expressed through facial expressions and body movements. We convey another 38 percent primarily through our tone of voice. We deliver only 7 percent of our communications through actual words.

That's hard to believe, isn't it? But research indicates, and our own experiences confirm, that non-verbal communication – body language and tone – are far more powerful influences on behavior than words.

Imagine that you're being introduced to someone who says, "I'm delighted to meet you." That sounds pleasant enough. But imagine further that this person stands with folded arms, makes no eye contact, and talks in a deadpan tone. Which do you believe – the person's *verbal* or *non-verbal* communication? Tone and body language trump words every time.

SPEAK UP

Effective communication is a process that can be learned. It's an art that must be practiced. Here are three key principles you can immediately apply to improve the effectiveness of your communication:

⊙ **Keep your thoughts organized and speak slowly enough to be understood.** This rule seems obvious, but it's vital. Other people can't understand and respond to you if they don't hear what you say.

⊙ **Keep it short and simple (KISS).** When it comes to speaking, more isn't better. Say it succinctly, close your mouth, and listen to the other person. As Robert Greenleaf said, "Many attempts to communicate are nullified by saying too much."

⊙ **Make sure your verbal and non-verbal communications are aligned.** Saying one thing with your words and another with your body language and tone of voice causes confusion and mistrust. Be aware of the non-verbal messages you are sending, and make sure they are in agreement with your spoken language.

LISTEN UP

If you want to be a better communicator, learn to be a better listener. Abide by the 80/20 rule. Listen

80 percent of the time and talk only 20 percent of the time.

Good listeners are rare; they stand out in a crowd. "Most people never listen," observed Ernest Hemingway.

If you learn to listen well, others will notice. They will be more willing to trust your opinions, comply with your requests, take you into their confidence, and entrust you with responsibility:

To dramatically improve your listening skills, practice these four proven techniques:

⊙ **Listen to comprehend.**

  In our fast-paced society, very few people slow down enough to really hear what others are saying. In order to be a good communicator, listen with both ears.

⊙ **Listen with focus.**

  If you're conversing with someone who repeatedly looks over your shoulder, you don't feel respected or heard, do you? Be attentive. Listen with focus and respect. Concentrate on what the other person is saying, not on how you are going to respond.

⊙ **Listen without judgment.**

When you listen with openness, you engender feelings of support and mutual respect. Intentionally develop the ability and desire to accept new ideas. You'll increase both the effectiveness of your communication and the depth of your knowledge.

⊙ **Listen with sensitivity.**

Non-verbal communication is powerful and important. Pay attention to tone and body language. Listen "between the words." Often what's not said is more important than what is said.

COMMUNICATE IN STYLE

Communication styles vary from person to person. You will communicate more effectively when you adapt your approach to fit your listeners' temperaments.

For example, when talking with "task-oriented" people who exhibit a more formal demeanor, get straight to the point. Establish rapport quickly and stick to business. Be brief, clear, and specific.

If possible, organize your thoughts in advance and support your positions with facts. Logical thinkers can become tense, even irritated, if you wander off topic and engage in casual "chit-chat."

On the other hand, when communicating with "people-oriented" individuals, establish a strong personal connection before getting down to business. If you rush ahead with your agenda too quickly, you'll push these people away. Present your case softly, warmly, and conversationally. Ask questions to draw out comments and feelings. Be patient and let the conversation evolve to the desired outcome.

AN ENCOURAGING STORY

This story about a company with significant communication problems will give you additional insights and encouragement.

When the owner called me for help, he confessed that he didn't know what was causing the epidemic of misinformation and poor performance in his office. Relationships among his five employees were tense and disrespectful.

After interviewing each employee privately, I

called a company meeting. In keeping with my role as a coach, I encouraged them to develop their own solutions. "You're all talented individuals," I told them, "but you're not working well as a team. I want to ask each of you to take responsibility and not point fingers. What do you think we should do to fix this problem?"

Perhaps because they viewed me as an objective outsider, I was in a better position than the owner of the business to facilitate honest interaction. Gradually, people started to open up. One person in the group confessed that she perceived another to be rude. "She doesn't look up from her computer when I ask her questions," she complained.

"I hate interruptions," the other person admitted. But then she suggested, "I'll be glad to answer your questions if you simply ask me to come to your desk when I have a moment."

When I was visiting this company one week later, I could sense that tensions had eased. An employee confided to me, "I can't believe the difference in the atmosphere. We're more productive and we're actually having fun!"

Obviously, I was very encouraged by that feedback. I was even more encouraged when I visited the company one month later, and the woman who had admitted in the meeting that she resented interruptions pulled me aside.

"You may not know it," she confided to me, "but that dialog you facilitated had a huge impact on my life. I hadn't realized before how my behaviors affected other people. Now I'm more aware of how I come across, and I'm changing the way I relate. People have told me that I'm different, and I really feel different. Things are going better at work and at home. Thank you for helping me."

Wow! I love to see people gain new insights and grow. Honest communication precipitates a shift in perceptions that brings attitudes and behaviors to the conscious level. When individuals choose to take responsibility for change, the outcome is improved performance and increased success.

As a result of the communication process I facilitated, the employees in this company gained a new appreciation for their own communication styles and the communication styles of others. They also learned to take responsibility for their actions. This resolved some immediate issues and will help them avoid or solve similar problems in the future.

ONE MORE ENCOURAGING STORY

As we close this chapter, I want to tell you an encouraging story about another business with serious communication problems. Relationships between this company's five employees in middle management and the four lower-level employees were tense, uncooperative, and at times hostile.

"How can we solve these problems?" I asked the nine employees in a meeting that I called at the request of the owner. "Let's discuss what's going wrong so we can put it behind us and move forward."

The middle mangers began to talk. They acknowledged they were partly at fault, and they made a few suggestions.

But the lower-level employees said absolutely nothing! They refused to take advantage of this opportunity to clear the air. Perhaps they were fearful they would be punished if they risked being honest. As the meeting ended, nothing seemed resolved. I left feeling a bit discouraged.

When I returned to this company two weeks later, I expected to encounter the same hostile environment. You can imagine my surprise when the owner approached me smiling. "Since that meeting two weeks ago, one middle-management person has quit and all the others have begun talking to each other and being more open. People are commenting that they actually enjoy coming to work because they feel like a team!"

Our straight-forward, non-judgmental dialog had prompted an unhappy employee to face her own issues and make a decision. The company benefited, and she benefited. She's now much happier working in another job that better suits her skills and interests. Honest communication grounded in acceptance of personal responsibility fostered positive actions.

Self-expression must pass into communication
for its fulfillment.

PEARL S. BUCK

Chapter Eleven:

Drawing Strength From The Crowd

Athletic teams perform better before hometown fans. Runners pick up the pace when cheered on by the crowd.

In order to be successful in life, you also need to draw strength from the crowd. You need support from others.

In Chapter 12 we will talk about how you can benefit from support through accountability. In this chapter you'll learn how to boost your success by harnessing the power of networking.

Networking is –

⊙ A **process** of gathering and disseminating information and establishing connections to produce desired results.

⊙ An **attitude** that regards giving to and receiving from others as an essential tool for successful living that everyone can naturally and effectively utilize.

You already use networking in many areas of your life, often without thinking about it. When you seek advice from others as you search for good doctors, babysitters, schools, places to eat, and books to read, you're networking. When you help others find resources to fill their needs – in fact, anytime you give and receive information to make connections – you're networking.

Networking is an essential tool in the kit of every professional. In order to meet new people and maximize your personal and professional success, you need to learn to utilize this powerful technique. To illustrate this point, here are just a couple of areas where networking will give you a powerful advantage:

- ⊙ **Sales**

  For cultivating new business, personal referrals are approximately 80 percent more effective than cold calls, and they're far more cost-effective than advertising. Personal referrals developed through networking will open doors to new opportunities and usher you into the confidence of others, even total strangers.

- ⊙ **Job hunting**

  It's estimated that only 20 percent of employment opportunities are advertised, and that 80 percent of job-seekers go after those jobs. Those are poor odds! Networking puts you on the inside track to learn about and interview for the other 80 percent of job openings even before they're advertised. Statistics show that approximately 60 percent of all job openings are filled through networking!

For these and other reasons, I submit that you will be much more successful if you master and employ this powerful technique!

MAKE NETWORKING A PRIORITY

Many business executives neglect networking because they're "too busy." That's a mistake! Networking is a key to long-term success. Make time for networking now, even when you're busy, because relationships take time to develop. Don't wait until you're running low on new business leads and contacts. Keep the "funnel filled" by networking regularly and consistently.

Others neglect networking because they feel uncomfortable talking with strangers. That's another mistake! Even introverts can learn to enjoy and profit from networking.

Effective networking starts with the right attitude. Intentionally cultivate and practice the unselfish desire to build relationships in order to help others, as well as yourself. One of the key benefits of networking is the joy and satisfaction you will experience as you contribute to the lives of others and receive from them in return.

Your fears will subside when you focus on helping others. And your joy will escalate when you see how networking accelerates your success. So be prepared at all times to present yourself and your story to others.

DON'T KEEP SCORE

Make it your goal to serve other people by providing helpful information, even if they don't reciprocate. Think about what more you can do for them, not about what they owe you. Give referrals even when you receive none in return. Your unselfishness will be rewarded over time.

Because of the nature of my work, I've been able to refer quite a bit of business to one particular high-tech firm in my area. Although the owner of this firm never had the opportunity to reciprocate, I didn't keep score.

Recently, I asked his advice about a rather significant technical project I was working on. He did more than answer my question; he arranged for a technical expert to take care of it! In fact, he was delighted to have an opportunity to help me because of my past kindnesses to him.

When you give without thought of receiving, almost invariably your generosity will return to you in some way. One of the richest rewards of unselfishness is that you will become a person whom others want to know.

VALUE STATEMENTS

No matter where you go, one of the first questions people ask is, "What do you do?" You need to be able to answer that question succinctly and persuasively. That's where your value statement comes in.

A value statement captures in one sentence the essence of what you do to serve others. It describes the *value* you provide, not the *activities* you pursue.

For example, if you're a real estate agent and someone asks you what you do, don't simply say, "I sell houses." A better value statement would be, "I help people find the homes of their choice." Or if you're an insurance broker, your value statement might be, "I help people gain peace of mind by protecting them against catastrophic loss."

When people ask me what I do, I don't just reply that I'm a business coach. My value statement is, "I help businesses improve financially, and I help people improve their performance."

A good value statement serves as the catalyst for further dialog. When your value statement is genuine and well-articulated, people you share it with will typically respond, "How do you do that?"

Value statements are valuable tools for success. Refine and rehearse yours until it produces the results you want.

BUILDING RELATIONSHIPS

Maximize the results of your networking efforts by using the principles below to build relationships:

⊙ **Stay in touch**

Demonstrate your care for people and let them know they're on your mind by staying in touch. Utilize your imagination to express your interest and support in unique ways.

For example, you might want to send someone a newspaper or magazine article of interest and enclose a personal note. Acknowledge people's birthdays by calling, e-mailing or sending a card. Invite people to events you sponsor or plan to attend. Staying in touch builds relationships that over time lead to increased business success.

⊙ **Use "nurture marketing" to stay connected**

Make sure the people you want to build and maintain relationships with see or hear your name through at least three different modes of communication, such as phone calls, e-mails, cards, letters, press releases, newsletters, and advertising specialty products with your firm's name on them. A newsletter (either e-mail or regular mail) is an extremely effective way to stay in touch.

⊙ **Seek to develop strategic alliances**

Strategic alliances are mutually beneficial relationships you develop with individuals and organizations that provide products or services to the same audience you target. For example, if one of your target markets is the financial services industry, you might want to establish relationships with lawyers, accountants, and insurance brokers you respect. Because you all serve clients in this industry from different perspectives, you are ideally suited to make continuing referrals to each other.

Intentionally seek to build strategic alliances to reap a steady source of highly qualified referrals. As you develop these relationships, be selective and make sure you align yourself with competent people.

FROM WALLFLOWER TO WONDER WOMAN

As we close this chapter, I want to encourage you with a true story about one of my clients. When I first met Jane over two years ago, she had no self-confidence. I could tell that she was an incredible person, but she described herself as a wallflower. As you can imagine, her career selling consumer products was not skyrocketing.

"I hate networking," Jane admitted to me. "When I ask people for things, I always feel like I'm being too pushy."

"You've got it backwards," I told her. "Start focusing on what you can give to others rather than on what you can get. When you want to help others, they'll want to help you."

As I coached Jane over a two-year period on the principles presented in this book, she started to gain confidence. She lost weight and felt more comfortable just being herself. Over time she no longer avoided networking opportunities; she actually sought them out. As she began to excel in networking, her sales increased exponentially.

Recently I received a phone call from Jane. "Joan, you won't believe what happened! I just got back from a presentation on networking. There were over seventy-five people in the audience, and the speaker singled me out five times as an example of an outstanding networker. She called me a superstar! I was so overwhelmed that I had tears in my eyes."

If Jane can harness the power of networking and have fun doing it, so can you!

Coming together is a beginning;
Keeping together is progress;
Working together is success.

HENRY FORD

Chapter Twelve

Pacing Yourself

hampion marathoners pace themselves. They watch for the mile-markers, note their times, and adjust their speed as necessary in their race toward the finish line.

In life, your goals serve as your mile-markers, providing direction and motivation. But goals alone are not sufficient. You also will need to establish formal accountability systems so you can pace yourself.

THE IMPORTANCE OF ACCOUNTABILITY

Accountability facilitates success because it enables you to honestly evaluate your progress and adjust your actions to improve your performance. Accurate assessments facilitate learning and growth.

Well-designed accountability structures provide feedback on motives and behaviors that is objective, supportive, and beneficial. As someone once said, "More people would learn from their mistakes if they weren't so busy denying them."

Feedback still occurs when individuals and organizations fail to set up formal accountability systems, but it tends to be informal and haphazard. Rather than being objective, positive, and supportive, it risks being personal, condemning, and disruptive.

In the absence of formal accountability, some people are too hard on themselves. They maintain unrealistically high expectations that create unnecessary pressures and actually hamper their performance. Others are too easy; they let things slide that should be addressed.

This book presents many good strategies. But good strategies that don't prompt action are useless. To get better results in your life – and I'm assuming that's why you're reading this book – you'll need to turn your strategies into actions. If you merely continue to do what you've always done, you'll continue to get what you've always got.

Accountability prompts action. As the saying goes, "People do what you *inspect*, not what you *expect*." Margaret can testify to that.

When Margaret first became my coaching client, she had an extremely negative attitude. She was stuck in a job she didn't' like, and her personal life was less than satisfactory. After we worked together for a few months, she set some goals for herself. But weeks and months went by, and she didn't act on them.

Then, slowly but surely, she started to take hold of her life. One day I asked her what had prompted her to start working on her goals. She replied, "I knew I would be meeting with you."

Strictly speaking, coaches don't hold their clients accountable. We help them surface their own explanations for why they failed to accomplish their goals and fulfill their commitments. Then we support them as they examine their motives, transform their behaviors, and move forward.

In Chapter 1, you may remember meeting Roger, the president of the financial services firm. He's continued his coaching relationship with me primarily because he wants accountability. His firm is experiencing increasing success largely because he values our regular meetings and welcomes my questions.

At one of my regular monthly meetings at a medium-size company, the owners expressed concern because they had lost $50,000 the month before. I asked what projects had caused the loss, and they admitted they didn't know.

When I returned one month later for another meeting, the owners greeted me with smiles. "We made a profit of $120,000 last month!" they exclaimed. When I asked how they did it, they replied, "We knew you'd be asking questions, so we dug into the books, found out what projects were giving us problems, and made some changes."

Just as the goal-setting process promotes sound planning, the accountability process stimulates effective actions.

THE TEMPTATION TO AVOID ACCOUNTABILITY

In general, people don't eagerly seek accountability. Winton Churchill accurately captured the feelings most of us have toward accountability when he said, "I'm always ready to learn, although I do not always like being taught."

Entrepreneurs are often fiercely independent, highly creative people. Perhaps one reason they strike out on their own is because they don't like being restricted and "under someone else's thumb." If you're an entrepreneur, beware! You're especially vulnerable to the dangerous temptation to avoid accountability. After all, you're the boss, and you can avoid accountability if you want to.

Many start-ups fail because entrepreneurs did not set up the structures necessary to constrain their actions within the guidelines of their business plans. Businesses that do set up formal accountability structures significantly increase their probability of success.

ESTABLISHING ACCOUNTABILITY STRUCTURES

There are many different ways to establish accountability. For some people the best solution is an "accountability partner." That could be a friend who agrees to meet you at the gym or health club on a regular basis so you won't be tempted to miss your workouts. Or it might be someone who meets regularly with you so you can hold each other accountable to your business and/or personal goals.

Some married couples hold each other account-able for their family financial goals. They meet regularly, perhaps monthly, and review actual expenses compared to budget. Others I know find it helpful to get an outside perspective, so they ask their financial advisor to hold them accountable.

Many people ask coaches to help them with accountability. Coaches are well-equipped for this purpose because their training and skills, enriched by with their experiences with many other clients, enable them to ask insightful questions and provide non-judgmental, growth-producing support.

Other people participate in accountability groups that meet regularly to hold their members accountable. These groups often generate creative ideas when opportunities and challenges surface.

Use your creativity to build accountability struc-tures that best suit your needs in the key areas of your personal and professional life. For example, the business that my husband and I own has an account-ability relationship with another company that provides similar services. We conference by telephone quarterly to review the performances of our companies compared to our goals. Annually we meet in person to refresh our business plans for the upcoming year.

Once you establish your accountability relationships, respect them. Give your accountability meetings high priority; don't let more "urgent" matters rob their place on your calendar. Adjust these relationships as necessary so they continue to work for you.

CELEBRATING THE VICTORIES

Maybe you've seen an incident like this on television: The sporting event has just concluded. Before the winner even catches his breath, the announcer asks, "How do you feel about your chances in your next event?"

I'm always delighted when the athlete replies, "Let me enjoy this victory first, before I think about the future." Too often we don't adequately enjoy our victories. We don't take time to savor our successes.

When you or others achieve significant goals, remember to celebrate! Make your victories more special and more real by acknowledging them publicly in an announcement in your newsletter, in an e-mail, or in the local newspaper. Reward yourself or the others involved with a dinner out, an afternoon off, or even a vacation.

If you're a manager, acknowledge those under your authority when they achieve individual and team goals. A simple word of praise goes a long way.

Too many managers are quick to point out failures and slow to applaud successes. Compliment people liberally and frequently, both privately and publicly.

One of my clients gives his employees quarterly bonuses when they meet their goals. That's good, but I've noticed that over time financial rewards tend to lose their appeal. His people have come to expect certain amounts, and now they want more. Be imaginative about the types of rewards you offer. Sometimes activities are better than money.

For example, another of my clients lets his office personnel create their own rewards. When the staff exceeded its goal of over three hundred patients per week for one quarter, they rewarded themselves with an outing to a professional football game. As the prize for achieving an annual goal, they decided on a trip to Bermuda. The freedom to set their own rewards has stimulated lots of excitement and creativity, and it has increased the motivational value of the program.

DON'T PROCRASTINATE

I hope I've persuaded you that goals should be coupled with systems of accountability. Goals provide direction and motivation; accountability prompts action and evaluation.

So, what are you waiting for? I'm holding you accountable to set up systems of accountability.

Remember, the purpose of accountability is not to find fault, but to help you find the path to success. Accountability, properly executed, replaces subjective criticism with objective feedback.

Don't be too hard on yourself when you fall short. Sometimes you may fail to accomplish a goal because deep down you don't think it's important. Accountability can provide the impetus for refocusing your priorities.

All individuals and organizations have room for growth. As someone once said, "The largest room in the world is the room for improvement." Accountability tied to goals provides constructive support for positive performance.

"If you want to know your past - look into your present conditions. If you want to know your future - look into your present actions."

CHINESE PROVERB

Chapter Thirteen:

Standing On The Podium

The winners of the Olympic race are standing on the podium with their gold, silver, and bronze medals draped around their necks. As the national anthem begins to play, tears trickle down the cheeks of the champion.

What thoughts lie beneath those deep emotions? The joy and satisfaction of accomplishment? Pride in representing one's country?

Gratitude for the many people who have given support and encouragement along the way? Memories of the journey, knowing now that the years of pain and sacrifice, from the "picking up of the first stone" to the attainment of victory, have been worth the effort? Probably all of those things and more.

You, too, will experience many of those same emotions as you celebrate your successes. The satisfaction of pursuing your passion and achieving your goals will fill you with joy and pride. You'll cherish the memories of the journey, with all of its struggles and rewards. And you'll be deeply grateful for the relationships you built along the way.

Yes, it's certainly better to stand on the podium than to be stuck in the starting blocks.

All worthy goals lie somewhere beyond what you know for certain is possible. If you want to mount the podium, you must confront and overcome the fear of failure.

If you decide to pursue your dreams, you *might* fail. But if you don't pursue your dreams, you *will* fail.

Failing to achieve all of your ultimate goals does not mean ultimate failure. Many of the things that matter most – strength of character and the sense of fulfillment that comes from doing your best – are derived more from the journey than from the destination.

Along the way you might stumble from time to time. But remember that you always can pick yourself up, prepare anew, and try again. As playwright Samuel Beckett said, "Ever tried. Ever failed. No matter. Fail again. Fail better."

Do you know that you can win the race? Are you convinced that you can realize your dreams? I hope so, because it's true. So, *Ready, Set, Plan, Go!*

During the opening ceremonies of the Olympic Games, the contestants recite the following:

I have prepared.
I have followed the rules.
I will not quit.

I hope you will use this book to *prepare* for greater success than you previously thought possible.

And I hope you will follow *rules* – the proven principles – set forth in this book so that you will accomplish all of your goals.

But most of all, I hope you will not *quit*. I hope you will blast out of the starting blocks and run your life's race with all the passion, energy, commit-

ment, and perseverance that is within you. I hope
you will run – and keep running – like the wind!

*Most people never run far enough on their first wind
to find out if they've got a second. Give your dreams
all you've got and you'll be amazed at the energy
that comes out of you.*

WILLIAM JAMES

How A Coach Can Help

J ust as good athletic coaching can help produce winning athletes, good business coaching can help produce successful professionals.

Coaches believe that the potential to succeed already resides within every individual; it simply must be uncovered, focused, and nurtured. Coaches do not have agendas or give advice. Rather, they seek to help their clients clarify their own goals and develop their own solutions. Most coaches would agree with Cicero who said, "No one can give you better advice than yourself."

The coach creates a safe place in which clients are free to share their hopes, dreams, goals, problems, and fears in complete confidence and without fear of judgment. By listening, encouraging, questioning, and challenging, the coach supports clients in becoming the best they can be.

In the supportive safety of the coaching relationship, clients increase their awareness of underlying desires and issues. They are then able to maximize performance in all areas of their lives by tapping into their innate potential, strengthening their abilities, and identifying and overcoming internal and external obstacles to success.

Before coaches can help clients get where they want to be, they must first help them see where they are. Individuals must increase their awareness in order to bring their passions, desires, attitudes, and behaviors to the conscious level. In effect, that was the primary purpose of Chapters 2 and 5 of this book.

After clients have identified their starting points by surfacing their passions, desires, attitudes, and behaviors, they can choose whether to take responsibility for their lives by setting goals and defining action steps toward accomplishing those goals. Chapter 4 and Chapters 6 through 13 dealt primarily with this phase of the coaching relationship.

Coaches are not therapists. They do not attempt to help their clients resolve issues from their past. Their role is to listen and to help clients visualize possibilities and make wise choices that lead to a balanced life of maximized performance and fulfillment. They are concerned with their clients' past only when past activities affect future performance.

Many of my clients utilize coaching as a follow-up to strategic planning or organizational development. When consulting and development is leveraged by coaching, individuals and organizations more effectively apply their new knowledge and skills to achieve maximum beneficial results.

More and more organizations are discovering the benefits of providing individual coaching to all, or substantially all, of the members of their management teams. Team coaching helps ensure that all members have the same vision and are committed to the same values and goals. Without violating any trusts or revealing confidential information, the coach can often ask questions that will help the people being coached to gain new insights and broader perspectives that lead to better decisions.

Coaching promotes personal growth through the transformation of perceptions and attitudes. Transformation produces positive changes in behaviors that are significant and lasting, resulting in increased performance and satisfaction in all areas of life.

Coaches delight in seeing their clients unleash the capabilities that are within them and achieve positive results that exceed their wildest expectations.

Appendix II

Recommended Resources

The resources listed below offer valuable knowledge, inspiration, tools, and techniques to accelerate your success. Of the many excellent resources on the market, I've found these to be especially useful. For easy reference, they are organized according to the sections of this book.

READY

Jack Canfield, *The Success Principles* **(New York: HarperCollins Publishers, 2004)** Affirms the importance of taking 100 percent responsibility for one's life, and provides twelve principles for increasing success.

Napoleon Hill, *Think and Grow Rich* **(New York: The Random House Publishing Group, 1937)** Tells how to overcome fear and achieve greater confidence, career advancement, and financial success.

Brian Tracy, *The Psychology of Achievement* **(New York: Simon and Schuster Inc., 1994)** Helps identify areas of personal excellence in one's life, as well as areas where change would result in greater success.

ASSESSMENTS

Assessment instruments increase self-awareness of personal strengths, behavioral patterns, natural abilities, and communications styles. Of the many excellent assessment instruments available, I am recommending the ones below because of their effectiveness and ease-of-use:

- ⊙ **DISC Profile** – a widely used and respected assessment tool for measuring behavioral styles. Awareness of behavioral styles facilitates more effective communication, which in turn leads to improved relationships and performance.

- ⊙ **The Birkman Method** – a multi-dimensional assessment tool that combines behavioral, motivational, and occupational data to unlock the hidden motivators that affect individual and team performance.

- ⊙ **360 Degree Feedback Surveys** – user-friendly surveys that enable the surveyor to obtain feedback from peers, superiors, and subordinates that is highly useful for improving performance.

If you're interested in contacting distributors for the above assessments, e-mail me at jwalsh@fsmi.us.

SET

Stephen R. Covey, *The Seven Habits of Highly Effective People* (New York: Simon & Schuster, 1989. A highly regarded proponent of principle-centered leadership espouses seven key habits that lead to personal and professional success.

John Maxwell, *Today Matters* (New York: Center Street, 2004) A respected management consultant offers insightful advice for making every day a masterpiece.

Rick Warren, *The Purpose Driven Life* (Michigan: Zondervan, 2002) Discovering one's purpose in life adds meaning, reduces stress, focuses energy, and simplifies decision-making.

Richard N. Bolles, *How to Find Your Mission in Life* (California: Ten Speed Press, 2000) The author of *What Color is Your Parachute,* the immensely popular career guidance book, addresses the important subject of finding one's place in the world.

PLAN

Jim Collins, *Good to Great* (New York: Harper Business, 2001) Informative observations about how "good" companies became "great" companies.

Peter F. Drucker, *The Effective Executive, The Definitive Guide to Getting the Right Things Done* (New York: HarperCollins Publishers, 1966) This classic management book presents sound principles that are just as timely today as when they were first introduced.

Michael E. Gerber, *E-Myth Revisited* (New York: Harper Collins Publishers, 1995) Thorough and thoughtful tips for working *on* one's business rather than *in* one's business.

Linda L. Martin and David G. Mutchler, *Fail-Safe Leadership* (Orlando, FL: Delta Books, 2001) Clear, straight talk about correcting the leadership challenges in organizations.

GO

David Allen, *Getting Things Done; The Art of Stress-Free Productivity* (New York: Penguin Books, 2001) Powerful methods to vastly increase one's personal organization, efficiency, and creative results – at work and in life.

Keith Ferazzi, *Never Eat Alone: And Other Secrets to Success, One Relationship at a Time* (New York: Doubleday, 2005) Valuable guidance about the power of networking, making connections, and building relationships.

Keith Harrell, *Attitude is Everything* (New York: HarperCollins Publishers, 2003) A practical guide for gaining control of one's life by developing positive attitudes and translating them into actions that will turn dreams into reality.

Jeffrey Gitomer, *Little Black Book of Connections* (Austin, TX: Bard Press, 2006) How to network one's way to a more profitable life.

WEB SITES

The websites below provide much useful information for professional growth, networking, and personal inspiration.

www.fastcompany.com – Hundreds of fascinating, informative articles about rapidly growing companies – what they do and how they do it.

www.ezinearticles.com – Insightful and useful articles about leadership, self-development, management development, and other success-oriented topics.

www.great-quotes.com – Quotes for inspiration and motivation, organized by subject.

www.BNET.com – A treasure trove of useful business whitepapers on various leadership and management topics.

www.linkedin.com – An on-line networking group that links participants with others who are also interested in networking.

ABOUT THE AUTHOR

Joan Walsh is a business coach. She is a co-founder and principal of FSMI, a firm that specializes in helping individuals and organizations create plans, set goals, and implement actions to achieve extraordinary success.

Through coaching and consulting, Joan assists clients in expanding their awareness, discovering their passion, increasing their confidence, and realizing their dreams. Her passion is supporting others as they seek to be all they can be.

Over her successful twenty-seven year career, Joan has worked in a variety of industries in the areas of strategic planning, marketing, sales, and organizational development. Prior to co-founding FSMI, she operated her own business and worked with Westinghouse Broadcasting Company, Sperry & Hutchinson, Time Inc., and Hallmark Cards.

Joan has an MBA and a Bachelor of Arts degree in English and Communications. Her dynamic personality makes her a popular speaker and facilitator. She and her husband, Tim, live with their two sons, Bobby and Brian, in Kennett Square, PA.

ABOUT THE COMPANY

FSMI helps businesses improve their financial results and individuals improve their performance. Co-founders Joan and Tim Walsh have over fifty years of combined experience helping their clients maximize their potential and achieve superior levels of success.

FSMI provides –

- ⊙ **Strategic planning** services to assist businesses in developing and executing plans to dramatically accelerate their growth and increase their profitability.

- ⊙ **Organizational development** services to equip individual and organizational clients with the skills, knowledge, and attitudes they need to achieve their goals.

- ⊙ **Business coaching** services that enable clients to experience transformation that results in extraordinary performance in all areas of their personal and professional lives.

FSMI has successfully served hundreds of clients in a variety of industries across the United States, ranging in size from entrepreneurs to multi-billion dollar corporations.

CONTACT INFORMATION

FSMI
106 Nathaniel Lane
Kennett Square, PA 19348
610.925.3713
jwalsh@fsmi.us
http://www.fsmi.us

JOURNAL

JOURNAL

JOURNAL

JOURNAL

JOURNAL

JOURNAL

JOURNAL

JOURNAL

JOURNAL

JOURNAL